In The Asking

Poetry From The Pages Of "In the Asking, I Changed"

Charrvi Singh

BookLeaf Publishing

India | USA | UK

Made with ❤ on the BookLeaf Publishing Platform
www.bookleafpub.in
www.bookleafpub.com

Dedication

This collection is dedicated to every version of myself...past, present, and future. To the younger me who kept asking questions even when the world wasn't listening. To the person I'm still becoming, and to every phase of life that shaped me along the way. Every story I lived contributed something to this journey. In many ways, this is a tribute to the process of becoming...one that continues to unfold.

Preface

This is the poetry edition of the book series, *In the Asking, I Changed.* It was born from the desire to share a glimpse...not of the answers, but of the questions that shaped the writing. These poems are drawn from deeper reflections within the books. They aren't direct excerpts, but rather fragments of thought and emotion that sit beneath each chapter. Writing the books has been a journey of transformation, and this smaller collection captures the quieter moments of that process. My hope is that as you read, you begin to ask your own questions too, and find comfort in knowing you're not alone in them. This is an invitation to pause, to feel, and to begin the conversation within yourself.

Acknowledgements

To my **mother**: thank you for being the constant support I never had to ask for. Your presence, belief, and quiet strength have carried me through every step of this process.

To the **two friends** who gave me the confidence to share my words when I doubted myself: thank you. You showed me that my voice had a place in the world, even before I believed it myself.

To **my past**, with all its weight and beauty, I owe everything. Without it, these questions would not exist.

And to you, **the reader**: thank you for being here. Even if we've never met, your presence means more than you know. I hope these pages meet you gently, and that something in them stays with you long after the last word.

1. Feels True?

What if the right thing doesn't feel so right,
and standing tall keeps you up all night?
What if truth is a colder fire,
burning away what we most admire?

Is it brave to speak, or kinder to wait?
Can silence heal, or does it create hate?
When two kinds of good pull us apart,
which one do we follow, and which do we guard?

Is it strength to hold or grace to bend,
to shift a rule for the sake of a friend?
What if no choice leaves you clean,
and right and wrong are both unseen?

Does the world reward a steady spine,
or punish the ones who draw their own line?
What if the cost of staying true
is losing a piece of the person you knew?

If values change when we are tired,
were they real or just admired?
Can we still call it integrity,
if it grows inside uncertainty?

In the quiet moments we defer,
are we wiser... or unsure?
What if the question's not who I should be,
but who I become when no one sees me?

In The Asking, **Can I change and still be me?**

2. Rule and Ripple?

Where does duty end...and care begin?
When rules are clear, but hearts are thin?
Is kindness a pause, or a kind of delay?
When is it right to step out of the way?

If the world runs on systems and time,
can we still hear the hurt between the lines?
When the chart says no, and the eyes say please,
which voice deserves the greater peace?

Do we break the rule to hold a hand?
Or follow through, just as planned?
When the numbers rise, but something feels wrong,
is it weakness to feel, or strength all along?

Can a single yes undo the frame,
built to keep the process sane?
And what do we lose, when we don't ask why,
when we walk on by, and call it "comply"?

When metrics matter more than pain,
do we become cold, or just humane?
Can one small grace unbalance the load,
or plant compassion where silence once showed?

What do we owe to the ones unseen,
whose stories slip through the space between?
When every choice leaves a bruise or a scar,
what kind of leader reveals who we are?

If fairness means ignoring the plea,
am I fair... or just afraid to see?
When I choose the rule, what do I trade...
and who am I, once that choice is made?

In The Asking, **Can I carry both the rule and the ache...
and still feel whole?**

3. Spark Is Silent?

What is motivation...truly, at heart?
A fleeting spark, or a conscious start?
Does it live in dreams, in coffee, in light,
Or come like thunder in the middle of night?

Is it discipline's twin, or emotion's guest?
Does it visit when we're feeling our best?
Or does it arrive in ordinary clothes,
On days when nothing in us glows?

Is it wrong to wait for the "right" kind of fire...
The perfect mood, the surge, the burning desire?
Or can small steps count when passion is gone,
Like showing up quiet, just moving along?

Can motivation grow from care, not thrill
From knowing, not feeling, we must climb that hill?
Can it sit beside grief, or borrow from peace?
Can it whisper through silence and still not cease?

Why does it vanish when we need it the most?
Why do we scroll and stall and ghost?
Are we lazy... or just worn thin?
Is it fear of failure that cages us in?

What if motivation isn't loud or bold,
But a hand we hold when the morning feels cold?
What if it's not something to chase or find,
But something that softens when we're kind?

Can we show up out of love, not force
Not dragged by guilt, but gently, of course?
And if we rest when the spark feels slow,
Is that quitting...or letting something grow?

So when you're tired and stuck in place,
Not broken, just out of your usual grace
Ask not, "Where is my will today?"
But "What do I need to feel okay?"

In the Asking, **Can care itself be what lights the way?**

4. Job of Becoming?

What shapes the work we choose?
A spark, a need, a borrowed voice?
Is a calling always clear, or quietly cobbled together
from late nights and what-ifs?

Do we chase passion or permission?
Do we build toward something
or away from what we fear?

Is purpose something we uncover,
or something we pretend to feel
until it finally fits?

Why must we name a destination
before we've learned how to walk without maps?

What if ambition isn't always loud
what if it sits softly, waiting to change its shape?

Can uncertainty be its own kind of compass?

Can delays be directions?

Is success still success
if it brings no joy?
Is work still worth doing
if it asks too much of who we are?

What if the goal isn't to arrive,
but to keep becoming?
Not one thing,
but many versions of honest effort?

Are we failing, or simply unfolding?

Is there shame in questioning
what the world demands we pursue?

If worth isn't in titles,
where does it live?

In The Asking, **What if becoming was the work all
along?**

5. Mirror Too Sharp to Hold?

What makes a body worthy of grace?
Is it in its curve, its size, its face?
Do we need approval just to be
At peace with who we dare to see?

Why do glances speak so loud,
While words disguise their shame in proud
"Just care," they claim, or "friendly tips,"
But wound us deep with tightened lips?

Who decided thin was best,
Or called a stomach rest unblessed?
When did comfort lose its charm,
And clothes become a ground for harm?

Can joy exist without a filter?
Can pride in skin survive the silt of
"Too much here" or "not enough"?
How did being soft become so tough?

Do mirrors lie, or do we bend
To what we think we must defend?
Why must we shrink to feel okay
Erase the bold to ease the gaze?

Why is silence praised in pain,
While laughter draws critique again?
Why can't a body's simple grace
Be something time is free to trace?

Must movement mean performance, too
Or is it joy when breath is true?
Can stretch marks, scars, and shifting weight
Be seen as life and not as fate?

Do you remember who you were
Before a comment made you blur?
Before the voice inside your head
Repeated all the things they said?

What if worth was not assigned?
Not whispered, shamed, or redefined?
Could beauty be a gentler sound
A quiet pulse, a sacred ground?

In The Asking, **What if your body was never the problem to begin with?**

6. If You Knock?

What is a boundary
a border, a break, or a quiet plea?
Is it harsh, or is it tender,
a gentle way to say: see me gently, not freely?

Is "no" always rejection, or sometimes a grace,
a whisper that says: this is my space?
Why does love stretch only one way,
expecting our yes at the end of each day?

Can I guard my joy without guilt in my tone?
Can I claim my hours and still not be alone?
Why do people flinch when we draw a line,
as if care must mean: always say you're mine?

Is it selfish to pause, to take a step back?
Or can stillness be strength, not something we lack?
Why do we doubt what discomfort tells,
And wait for it to grow before it swells?

Must closeness demand my constant reply?
What if I need silence and still qualify
as loving, as loyal, as deeply aware
what if boundaries are just how I care?

Can I be kind and still say no?
Must I explain each place I won't go?
Why is the lock seen as a threat, not relief?
Why does clarity summon disbelief?

What would change if children were taught
that kindness means knowing what cannot be bought?
That their bodies, their voices, their peace are their own
not gifts to be borrowed, not lands to be known?

Can we stop assuming access is earned
by how well someone waits, or how long we've
returned?
What if "too much" was just someone's fear,
and I'm allowed to be full, to take up space here?

What does it mean to be seen and not used?
To speak and not be accused or refused?
To let love enter only through doors that unlock
and say: you are welcome... but only if you knock?

In The Asking, **What if the truest love begins at the threshold of "no"?**

7. Colour?

What if colours see us first,
long before we claim or curse?
Do they rise like morning skies,
or sink with truths we won't reprise?

Does red demand, or does it plea
a burning blush, a quiet see?
Is blue a balm or distant sigh,
a held-back tear we dress in sky?

What shades do aching fingers find
when comfort lags a step behind?
Which tones do we no longer wear
because they knew us when we cared?

Is pink still soft if worn with rage?
Can gold outgrow its gilded cage?
And black, so feared, so sharp, so deep
does it not guard the dreams we keep?

Who said that lavender was brave,
or navy meant we must behave?
Why must the sun stay yellow, still
when children paint it by their will?

Why do we colour grief in grey,
and love in red that fades away?
Do hues remember what we lost
each joy dismissed, each line we crossed?

Do we dress for who we are,
or for approval from afar?
Is olive peace or camouflage?
Can violet speak without barrage?

And when we mix the tones anew,
what parts of self come breaking through?
Is this not art—this pulse, this skin
each shade a place we've never been?

In The Asking, **What truths begin when colour steps in?**

8. Louder Than Silence?

A word is not just breath and sound
it builds, it bends, it breaks, it binds.
Some settle soft like roots in ground,
some echo sharp in tangled minds.

Not all loud things make a noise.
Not all silence is a choice.
A single phrase, both kind and brief,
can plant a seed or steal belief.

Why do we speak as if words weigh none,
when hearts still bruise from what was done?
Why dress a knife in jest's disguise,
then wonder why the laughter dies?

What tone do we leave in a room behind?
What dust of thought, what shape of mind?
Is urgency excuse enough
to trample through and call it tough?

What if our language shaped the air,
like scaffolds built from quiet care?
Would we be slower, gentler still
less steel command, more open will?

Can truth exist inside a plea?
Can strength arrive more tenderly?
Must power always sharpen its edge,
or can it whisper, break its pledge?

We name ourselves with what we say
the scripts we chant, the words we weigh.
So if we shift the lines we keep,
what parts of us might rise from sleep?

In The Asking, **Can kindness be as clear as command?**

9. Numbing Noise?

We think we choose our thoughts each day,
But how much choice lives in the fray?
Between the swipes, the scrolls, the trends,
Where does the self begin or end?

The feed repeats what feels like "me"
A hall of mirrors, endlessly.
Each echo smooths the rough away,
Till all dissent has gone astray.

Do we still crave what's deep, what's real?
Or just what's packaged, primed to feel?
A joke, a jingle, something bright
Not crafted truth, just clickbait light.

When did absurd become enough?
When did we trade in depth for fluff?
We follow noise, we mimic tone,
Yet somehow still feel more alone.

Does friction scare us into mute?
Do we confuse the loud with truth?
What price we pay for every nod
A borrowed thought, a silenced God.

If comfort's all we seek and share,
Then who will dare to speak what's rare?
To choose the pause, the slower pace,
To think beyond a trending face.

Are we just watching others play,
Afraid to mean what we might say?
And if we echoed something new,
Would it still matter, still feel true?

In The Asking, **And what if clarity begins in quiet?**

10. Doors Too Many?

So many doors, and none feel right
Too bright, too loud, too dim, too tight.
We stand and scan, then stand some more,
Exhausted by the open door.

We wanted freedom, skies to chase,
Not silence in an endless maze.
Is this the gift of having say
Or just the fear of choosing "stay"?

One path feels bold, the next feels safe,
Another whispers, just in case.
Each option echoes some regret,
Not for what is...but what we let.

We ask for time, we ask for signs,
We make decisions into shrines.
We hold our breath at every gate,
Afraid to love, afraid to wait.

But what if wrong is not a curse?
What if we're meant to choose...then learn?
What if the weight we try to bear
Is simply proof we deeply care?

We've made perfection our desire,
Then wonder why we all feel tired.
The right life isn't always clear
It just becomes so when we're here.

Do we forget, when weighing fate,
That meaning comes a second late?
Not as we choose, but as we stay
And shape the hours along the way.

In The Asking, **What if the wrong door still leads us home?**

11. Remembered?

What does it mean to be remembered?
Is it kindness... or command?
Is it the heart behind an action,
Or just the mark it leaves on land?

Does the world reward what's noble,
Or simply what it sees?
Is greatness found in goodness,
Or in bending history's knees?

We say that right will echo,
But echo isn't proof.
Sometimes it's just repetition
Not morality, just truth...
Made louder.

If power writes the narrative,
Who holds the pen of grace?
Can silence still be virtue
If it never finds a place?

What do we honor in leaders
Their wisdom or their might?
Do we measure their legacy
By ethics... or by height?

If virtue must shout to matter,
Was it virtue all along?
And if justice feels forgotten,
Does that mean the loud are strong?

Are we building toward integrity,
Or just toward being known?
Is legacy a mirror,
Or a shadow we disown?

Does goodness lose its meaning
When no one stops to see?
And if fame outlives our choices,
Are we ever truly free?

In The Asking, **Do we chase impact... or integrity?**

12. Disappearing? Loving?

Is love a shelter or a stage?
A promise or a gilded cage?
We speak of choice with lifted chin,
But does the choosing ask us to shrink within?

What does it mean to say "I do,"
If doing means undoing you?
If love is meant to help us grow,
Why are we the first to go?

Why does warmth come with a weight,
A script of silence, dressed as fate?
Why must devotion always prove
That duty is the price of love?

Who tends the tender once she's tired?
Why must her light be self-retired?
Why does care mean fading slow,
Until she's someone he used to know?

She gave, and gave, and called it grace
But who remembered her own face?
Why is sacrifice still crowned,
While her small joys are never found?

Is marriage still a sacred space,
Or just a softer kind of brace?
Does partnership mean mutual flight,
Or just one wing lost to make it right?

What if love was not a test,
Of how much less makes you your best?
What if vows were not demands,
But gentle, open, outstretched hands?

In the Asking, **Can love hold her without making her vanish?**

13. What To Name This Ache?

Why do some goodbyes wear no sound,
No slam of doors, no battleground?
Why do the closest ones we knew
Drift quietly, until they're through?

Why does silence feel like theft,
When no one fought, and yet you're left?
Why do the friendships built so deep
Slip into shadows we can't keep?

Is time to blame for hearts undone?
Or are we all just on the run
From reaching out, from saying more,
From wondering what we're sorry for?

When did we trade long midnight talks
For birthday texts and virtual walks?
When did "always" lose its glow,
Becoming "sometime" said too slow?

They're not gone, they just don't call.
And that might hurt the most of all.
No betrayal, no sharp refrain
Just the soft echo of old names.

Can someone vanish while still near?
Can they forget what we held dear?
How do we mourn the friends who stay,
But turn their faces the other way?

Why do I scroll, still half in hope
That something typed could help us cope?
That "I miss you" might rewind time
Back to when "us" still felt like mine?

I carry laughter no one hears,
Inside my chest like phantom years.
Is this what love becomes with age
A bookmark on a fading page?

In the Asking, **Can love endure even after it goes quiet?**

14. Sorry?

Why do we rush to name the ache,
With words that tremble, thin, and break?
Why is silence such a fear
That we must speak to feel sincere?

What does "I'm sorry" really do,
When grief is wide and words are few?
Is it comfort, is it grace
Or just a way to fill the space?

When sorrow rises, raw and deep,
Why do we offer lines to keep
The moment safe, the silence sealed,
Instead of asking what's revealed?

Do we listen just to speak,
Or to hold the truths they cannot speak?
Must every sadness wear a tag,
A script, a nod, a softened flag?

Is care a phrase we overuse,
When presence would be more of use?
Why does empathy arrive so fast
Too polished, too rehearsed to last?

What if not all pain wants cure,
Not every wound needs to endure
Another voice, another thread
What if it only asks to be read?

Is sorrow asking to be solved,
Or simply not to be dissolved?
Must we respond to every cry,
Or can we learn just to sit nearby?

In The Asking, **When did we forget that silence can hold?**

15. Almost?

What do we do with the words unsaid,
The ones that echo inside our head?
The questions paused upon the tongue,
The thoughts we silenced, young and hung?

Do they dissolve, or do they stay,
Shadows we carry day by day?
Why does silence bruise the chest,
Louder than voices we confessed?

Are we guarding hearts with quiet grace,
Or just afraid to lose our place?
Is it kindness not to speak the truth,
Or fear dressed up in patience, couth?

Why does "next time" come too late,
A door unopened at the gate?
Can silence be a form of care,
Or just absence wrapped in air?

Are we more afraid to say too much,
Or not enough, or say and touch
A wound that time forgot to heal
What is more tender: truth or zeal?

Is love still love when never said?
Do words withheld become the thread
That binds regret to memory's spine
A haunting made of might-have-been lines?

In The Asking, **But what if the words were always meant to be said?**

16. Cost of Yes?

How many times do we nod and agree,
When our heart whispers quietly, "Let me be"?
How often is kindness a clever disguise,
For fear of rejection behind smiling eyes?

Where do we learn that peace must be earned,
That love requires our comfort unlearned?
Why does "no" feel heavy with shame,
While "yes" leaves us weary, never the same?

Is politeness a virtue or just a demand,
To shrink ourselves small, to lend out a hand?
What do we lose when we silence our voice,
And give every inch as though we've no choice?

They praise the ones who bend and give,
But who applauds the will to live
To rest, to breathe, to simply say,
"This is my boundary. Not today"?

Is love real if it wilts when we pause,
If it's only upheld by applause?
Does care require a yes every time,
Or can "no" also be tender, also be kind?

Do they stay because we serve and smile,
Or would they still love us after a while,
If we chose ourselves in quiet defiance,
If we answered their pull with honest compliance?

We are not endless, nor made of steel.
We too deserve to feel what we feel.
And when we say no, the world may not break
It might just shift, it might just wake.

How many times can we stretch before we snap?
Who are we when we take ourselves back?

In The Asking, **What if no was the beginning of love, not the end?**

17. Running? No, Moving

Why does the morning begin with a race,
Before we've even found our place?
Why must waking feel like a chase,
And stillness a luxury we can't embrace?

Who told us that tired is something to prize,
That worth is tallied in sleepless eyes?
When did we trade joy for pace,
And call it purpose, call it grace?

Why does rest come laced with guilt,
As if the world might crack or tilt?
Why must we prove we've earned our pause,
Instead of resting just because?

Are we more than what we do,
If we slowed down, would that still be true?
Is ambition only loud and fast,
Or can it whisper, breathe, and last?

What if success was not the climb,
But choosing peace and guarding time?
Why must hobbies earn a name,
A profit, a title, a touch of fame?

Can we live without the rush,
Without the noise, the endless crush?
Do we need to be in motion,
To deserve love, to earn devotion?

When did existing become a test,
And doing less mean we're less blessed?
Can silence be its own reward,
Not a gap to fill, but a resting chord?

Why must we break to finally see
That being is enough to be?

In The Asking, **What if stillness was never a weakness,
but a way back home?**

18. Doing Nothing?

Why does the quiet feel so loud,
As if stillness is something not allowed?
Why must every breath be traced,
Every pause somehow erased?

When did effort become our name,
And rest a cause for quiet shame?
Why does the void ask us to lie,
To fill it fast, not wonder why?

Why can't a moment simply be,
Without the urge to measure me?
Must time be useful to be real
Is presence something we must steal?

Why do we flinch when nothing calls,
As if the world might crack or fall?
Can rest exist without defense,
Not earned by sweat, but common sense?

Is silence something to outrun,
Or just the place we come undone?
Why does discomfort rise so fast,
When we're not anchored to a task?

Are we afraid to hear our minds,
Uncurated, undefined?
What if the work was not to do,
But to sit still, and make that true?

Who are we beyond the goal,
The calendar, the self-control?
What if the day was slow and bare
Would we find guilt, or freedom there?

Not everything must serve a plan.
Not every joy must serve demand.
And maybe we are most complete
When we are still, and feel our feet.

In The Asking, **What if being was enough to believe in?**

19. Never Became?

I grieve the echoes of silent plans,
Drawn in dust by unseen hands.
Not every dream dies loud and bold
Some simply slip, unlived, untold.

How many selves were stitched inside,
Woven in hope, then set aside?
Do we mourn them as we grow,
Or let them go, and never know?

What of paths that fade too fast,
Forks we missed, or chose to pass?
Did I surrender or evolve,
When who I was began to dissolve?

If I step outside the frame,
And leave behind that given name,
Am I a wanderer or released
From a promise never truly leased?

Can shedding skin be called regret,
When what remains is wiser yet?
Or is it grief that hides its face
In every silent, shifting place?

Who am I beyond the mold,
When no script remains to hold?
Is it loss or is it flight
To question every former right?

And if I am no longer her,
The one imagined, once so sure
Does that mean I've lost my way,
Or found a softer one today?

In The Asking, **Did I disappear, or finally arrive?**

20. Half-Healed?

They say to forgive is to set yourself free,
But what if the lock still clings to the key?
What if the wound knows how to behave,
Yet still aches in the quiet you gave?

Is grace still real if it's laced with a scar?
Can peace exist with pain not far?
Do I forgive when I speak it aloud,
Or only when silence no longer feels loud?

Can I let go without letting it fade?
Must the debt be repaid for amends to be made?
If I said "I forgive," but flinched at the sound,
Does it mean my healing is somehow unsound?

They want it to end like a well-written page,
But sometimes forgiveness lives under rage.
It isn't a ribbon tied neat at the end,
It's a line I redraw, again and again.

Must closure come wrapped in a perfect reply?
What of the questions that still make me cry?
If I moved on but the past still appears,
Am I a fraud for holding back tears?

Is it still forgiveness if anger remains?
Can a heart move forward while bearing old strains?
Or do I have space to feel both and still grow
To forgive, to remember, to learn, and let go?

Not every sorrow asks to be cured.
Some simply ask to be quietly endured.
But am I allowed to still feel the sting...

In The Asking, **Can I carry peace while still holding the pain?**

21. Silence Learned to Burn?

There's a kind of fire that makes no sound,
No spark, no blaze, no cracking ground.
It simmers low behind the eyes,
And smiles while hiding all its cries.

Is it rage that flares from nothing new,
Or is it sorrow dressed in hue?
Does anger rise when words fall short,
Of saying: I just need support?

Why do shoulders tighten in quiet pain,
When no one asked, again, again?
Why do voices break mid-sentence too,
When all we want is, "I see you"?

Do slammed doors say more than tears could tell?
Is loneliness the sound before we yell?
What if burnt toast or a traffic line
Are just disguises for "I'm not fine"?

Why do we mask what's underneath,
With sudden storms and silent grief?
Do we truly hate, or do we ache
For someone to notice what's at stake?

When did we learn to bark, not bleed,
To scoff at love, and silence need?
Is anger power, or just a shield
For softer wounds we've not revealed?

What sits behind the sharpened tone?
Is it fear of being left alone?
Why is it easier to shout than show
The truth we barely even know?

What do we miss when rage takes lead?
Is it connection? Care? Or simply need?
If someone paused and softly said,
"What pain still lives inside your head?"

Would we still rage... or would we weep?
Unravel all we tried to keep?
Would sorrow speak if given space,
To show its tired, tear-stained face?

So now I ask the heat within
What wound began this noise and din?

And every time I pause to see,
A softer voice returns to me.

It doesn't scream, it doesn't shout,
It whispers things I'd locked far out.
And in that quiet, there's no blame...
Just grief that never got a name.

In The Asking, **What has my anger been begging me to feel?**

22. Ordinary?

What if the stars were never ours to name?
What if we lived without glory or fame?
Would we still matter in quiet ways,
In whispered nights or unspoken praise?

Can a life be full when it's soft and small,
Not built to climb but to catch a fall?
What if the worth of a moment unseen
Outweighed a crown or a glowing screen?

Why do we chase what leaves us tired,
A borrowed dream we never desired?
Can kindness count when no one looks?
Can silence sing in unwritten books?

If all we are is someone's peace,
Not heroes, but a soul's release
Would that be less, or would that be more
Than breaking through a distant door?

Can the average heart be sacred ground?
Can beauty in the plain be found?
Is legacy made in gold or grace
In touching just one life, one place?

In The Asking, **What if being enough was the quietest form of greatness?**

23. Unwritten?

Why does the page so pure and wide
Feel more like cliff than open tide?
Why does its hush begin to shout
Of all we fear, of every doubt?

What if we fail before we start
A trembling hand, a cautious heart?
Why does the space that could be free
Feel more like chains than clarity?

Do endless paths make us forget
The single step we haven't met?
Why do we freeze when choice is vast
Held hostage by a future cast?

Is it the dream that dares too loud,
That makes us cower in the crowd?
Or is it that the cost of choice
Mutes the mind and steals the voice?

Can we still move without a map,
When every route could be a trap?
Does pressure bloom where hope once lay
Upon the altar of the day?

In The Asking, **What if the blankness isn't empty, but just waiting to believe in me?**

24. Dream and Day?

We build our hopes with threads of gold,
So sure the world will take its hold.
But dreams don't always touch the sky
Some falter low, some never fly.

What name do we give the hollow ache
When all we planted does not wake?
Is it failure, fate, or just delay
Or something softer, tucked away?

Do we expect the world to bend
To promises we don't defend?
And when it doesn't shape our view,
Do we mourn what never grew?

Can something still be beautiful
If it remains unfinished, dull?
Can we find worth in broken lines,
Or joy in what the heart declines?

What lives inside a dream unmet
A quiet grief or no regret?
And is it wrong to wish for more,
When wishing leaves a tender sore?

Is this the cost of hope too high
To live beneath a shrinking sky?
Or does the ache remind us still
That wanting more is part of will?

Is peace acceptance, soft and wide
Or settling dressed in gentler pride?

In The Asking, **Is disappointment just the echo of a
dream still calling?**

25. Versions of Truth?

Do memories blur to keep us whole,
A softened edge, a gentler role?
Is truth a thread that time distorts,
Woven through our private courts?

Do we recall what truly was,
Or what the heart now needs...because?
When silence filled what should've screamed,
Did we rewrite the way it seemed?

Is it still lying if it saves
A younger self from deeper graves?
If pain was loud and joy was small,
Do we forget... or just recall?

How much do stories change to fit
The image we can sit with it?
Is memory a whispered grace
That shifts the facts to shield our face?

Did I exaggerate the fall,
Or was there never ground at all?
Do I now paint it with some light
Because the dark won every fight?

And when I tell it, eye to eye,
Do I believe each softened lie?
Is truth a duty we betray,
Or something we just shape our way?

Is it survival or deceit
To change the ending on repeat?

In The Asking, **What do we owe to the truth if it was never safe to speak it?**

26. "I'm Fine"?

How heavy is the quiet smile
That hides the storm for just a while?
Do we owe the truth a name,
Or is "I'm fine" the safer game?

What toll is paid with every nod
That masks the ache we never prod?
Do we pretend for peace or pride
Or fear what breaks when truth's applied?

How often do we choose the lie
Because we dread the wondering eye?
Can silence make us feel less weak,
Even when it's pain we seek?

What happens when the lies accrue
Each one a thread we're stitched into?
Is there a point the weight turns loud,
And all the soft pretenses crowd?

Do we believe we're kind to fake
The smile we force, the laughs we make?
Or do we cheat ourselves each day
By pushing all the hurt away?

Can love still hold what we conceal,
Or does it crack where we won't heal?
And if we whispered what was true,
Would that undo the version you knew?

Why do we fear the trembling voice
The one that doesn't leave a choice?

In The Asking, **What is the price of always seeming okay?**

27. Reaching Out?

Why do my hands forget to reach
When I have lessons I could teach
On how to hold and how to stay,
Yet stumble when I feel that way?

Is it weakness I disguise
Behind the calmness in my eyes?
Or shame that trails each quiet need,
While I keep tending others' seed?

If I give help without delay,
Why do I hide when I feel fray?
Is asking somehow less divine,
A flaw to tuck beneath the spine?

Do I believe I must be whole
To take up space, to bare my soul?
Who told me care should not return,
That love must flow one-way to earn?

What story taught me not to cry,
To wait till every tear runs dry?
Can I be held without a debt
Without a reason to regret?

What if the ones I lean upon
Are waiting too, with masks well-drawn?
Would my soft truth, if spoken clear,
Unravel all they've cloaked in fear?

Am I less worthy when I lean,
Less brave, less strong, less seen, less clean?
Or is it brave to say, "I'm not,"
To name the ache the world forgot?

What if in need, I'm still enough?
Not small, not shameful, not too much?

In The Asking, **Why is receiving harder than love itself?**

28. Too Late?

Why do the echoes find me now,
Long after I've unlearned the vow
To wait for someone else to see
The silent truths that once were me?

Why does praise arrive with dust,
After years of breaking trust?
Do they hear me more in loss
Than they ever did in chaos?

Why is clarity always delayed,
Admiration softly replayed
Only once I've left the stage
Now they reread every page?

Did I whisper too soon, too low?
Was I too gentle just to show
The thunder nested in my chest
Before they learned what I suppressed?

Is it easier to honour gone
Than to love what's still holding on?
Do we crown the quiet minds
Only after they resign?

Why do they need my absence there
To realise I was ever rare?
Was I meant to stand and wait
For their timing to translate?

When eyes awaken far too slow,
Should I return or let it go?
If worth arrives beyond the gate,
Does it still hold or come too late?

Was I loud enough in grace
Before I vanished from that place?

In The Asking, **Why do they always see us after we've gone?**

29. Conversations? Talking

Where did the heavy words go to hide,
The kind that shook the soul inside?
Did we trade depth for safer sound,
Afraid of truths that might confound?

Why do we fill the empty air
With phrases that don't even care?
Is silence now too loud to bear,
Too honest, too stripped, too rare?

Have we grown too used to noise,
Mistaking chatter for a voice?
When did we learn to skim, not dive
To seem alive, not feel alive?

Are we scared of what we'd find
If someone truly heard our mind?
Are shallow laughs a softer place
Than sharing what we dare not face?

Why do we flinch at the unseen
The quiet truths that lie between?
Is a paused breath more real than words
That flutter loud but go unheard?

Do we recall the last time we
Spoke of love or loss or memory
Without a screen, a script, a shield,
Without our truest thoughts concealed?

Is connection now a game,
Where keeping score outruns the name
Of everything we used to be
When silence sang so tenderly?

In The Asking, **When did we stop meaning what we say?**

30. Pink and Blue?

Who said pink is soft and blue is bold,
That warmth is weak and silence cold?
Who split the world in neat divides,
Then shamed the ones who crossed both sides?

Why must strength be laced with fight,
And softness fade into the night?
Can't muscle wear a tear with pride,
And kindness roar from deep inside?

Why is nurture seen as small,
And power praised when it stands tall?
What if the loudest hearts feel most,
And gentlest hands are not the ghost?

Must boys be rocks and girls the rain
One taught control, one taught refrain?
What if we're both, what if we shift,
What if these roles begin to lift?

Can a girl be more than grace and smile,
And still be loved, and still worthwhile?
Can a boy break down and still be brave,
Not hide his pain, not learn to cave?

Is gender just a well-worn mold,
Or something freer, something bold?
Are we reduced to pink and blue,
Or is there space for every hue?

Do we perform or do we feel
And which of these was ever real?
If hearts could speak, not just obey,
What truths would labels wash away?

In The Asking, **What if being ourselves was brave enough?**

www.ingramcontent.com/pod-product-compliance
Lightning Source LLC
Chambersburg PA
CBHW060351050426
42449CB00011B/2925